FUEL THE GROWTH OF YOUR BRAND

Your Guide To Mastering Google Ads

Dack Douglas

Icon Publications Limited

CONTENTS

FUEL THE GROWTH OF YOUR BRAND: YOUR GUIDE TO MASTERING GOOGLE ADS

INTRODUCTION

Welcome to "Fuel The Growth Of Your Brand: Your Guide To Mastering Google Ads." This book is specifically designed to help beginners understand and navigate the world of Google Ads without any prior knowledge or experience. Whether you're a small business owner, a marketer, or an aspiring digital advertiser, this book will provide you with a solid foundation to create effective Google Ads campaigns.

TABLE OF CONTENTS

- Conducting split tests to optimize campaigns
- Developing a continuous improvement plan for long-term success

CHAPTER 1: INTRODUCTION TO GOOGLE ADS

Understanding The Importance Of Google Ads

In the fast-paced and interconnected world we inhabit today, the importance of Google Ads cannot be overstated. At its core, Google Ads represents a gateway to a vast and diverse digital landscape, where businesses and individuals can tap into a global audience with unrivaled precision and reach. This digital marketing platform has revolutionized the way we connect with potential customers, transcending geographical boundaries and time zones to bring products, services, and ideas directly to the fingertips of those who seek them.

Google Ads is not merely an advertising tool; it is an intricate tapestry of insights, data, and algorithms that empower advertisers to navigate the digital realm strategically. It offers a unique opportunity to showcase brands, products, and messages in a visually compelling and contextually relevant manner, capturing the attention of consumers in the very moments they express interest or intent.

The brilliance of Google Ads lies in its adaptability, catering to the diverse needs and objectives of businesses, from startups to multinational corporations. It accommodates both modest budgets and ambitious campaigns, providing a level playing field for companies to compete and innovate. Whether you're a local entrepreneur seeking to expand your reach or a visionary aiming to launch a global sensation, Google Ads equips you with the tools and insights to make your mark on the digital stage.

In the world of advertising, relevance is paramount, and this is precisely where Google Ads excels. By harnessing the power of user behavior, intent signals, and sophisticated targeting options, it enables advertisers to serve their messages to the right audience at the right time. This personalization fosters a sense of connection and authenticity, cultivating long-term relationships between brands and consumers.

Moreover, the beauty of Google Ads is its capacity for continuous improvement. As campaigns unfold and data accumulates, advertisers can glean invaluable insights, unveiling what works and what doesn't. This iterative process fosters a culture of experimentation and growth, encouraging advertisers to refine their strategies and optimize their ads for maximum impact.

In a world inundated with information and choices, Google Ads stands as a beacon, guiding businesses towards the forefront of digital marketing. It beckons entrepreneurs and marketers to embrace the art of storytelling, to evoke emotions, and to captivate their audiences through the language of visuals and words.

As we venture further into the digital age, the importance of Google Ads will only grow, shaping the future of advertising and communication. Embrace its potential, and you'll discover a world of boundless opportunities to engage, inspire, and leave an indelible mark on the hearts and minds of those you seek to reach.

Overview Of The Google Ads Platform

At the heart of the ever-evolving digital marketing landscape stands the powerful and dynamic Google Ads platform. This ingenious creation by Google serves as an essential bridge, connecting businesses, advertisers, and organizations with a vast audience across the globe. In essence, Google Ads is a virtual marketplace where brands can showcase their offerings to potential customers, capturing attention at precisely the right moments when intent and curiosity converge.

At its core, Google Ads operates on a pay-per-click (PPC) model, offering a cost-effective and measurable approach to advertising. Advertisers bid on relevant keywords and phrases, determining when and where their ads will be displayed within Google's extensive network, including the search engine itself, partner websites, and apps. The system's intelligent auction mechanism ensures that ads are shown to users most likely to engage with them, fostering an environment of relevancy and efficiency.

One of the platform's standout features is its versatility, catering to businesses of all sizes and industries. From local brick-and-mortar stores to global e-commerce giants, Google Ads accommodates diverse goals and objectives, empowering advertisers to tailor their campaigns to suit their unique needs. The ad formats available range from text-based search ads that appear alongside search results to visually engaging display ads on partner websites and video ads on YouTube, captivating audiences through sight, sound, and motion.

Data lies at the heart of Google Ads, providing a treasure trove of insights that can transform campaigns from good to extraordinary. Advertisers can analyze performance metrics, track conversions, and measure the return on investment (ROI) with precision, facilitating data-driven decisions and optimizations. This constant cycle of analysis and refinement ensures that every dollar invested in advertising is maximized for impact and effectiveness.

Central to Google Ads' appeal is its audience-targeting prowess. Advertisers can define their target audience based on demographics, interests, online behaviors, and even specific actions taken on their websites. This laser-focused targeting fosters a sense of personalization, enabling brands to create messages that resonate deeply with their potential customers.

In the realm of digital marketing, adaptability is key, and Google Ads rises to the challenge. The platform continually evolves, introducing innovative features and tools to empower advertisers to stay ahead in an ever-changing landscape. From automated bidding strategies to responsive ads that adapt to different devices, Google Ads invites creativity and experimentation, beckoning advertisers to explore new possibilities and push the boundaries of their campaigns.

Ultimately, Google Ads represents more than just a platform; it symbolizes a boundless universe of opportunities for businesses to connect, engage, and thrive in the digital age. It embraces the spirit of innovation, harnesses the power of data, and celebrates the art of storytelling. As technology continues to advance and consumer behavior evolves, the journey within the realm of Google Ads remains an exhilarating expedition, promising endless discoveries and potential for those who dare to embark upon it.

Setting Up Your Google Ads Account

Setting up your Google Ads account is an exciting step towards unleashing the potential of online advertising for your business. Follow these original instructions to get started on your Google Ads journey:

1. Navigate to Google Ads: Begin by visiting the Google Ads website (ads.google.com) and click on the "Get Started" button to initiate the setup process.

2. Sign in or Create an Account: If you already have a Google account (e.g., Gmail), sign in with your existing credentials. Otherwise, create a new Google account, which will serve as the foundation for your Google Ads experience.

3. Identify Your Business Goals: Before proceeding, define your advertising objectives clearly. Whether it's increasing website traffic, generating leads, or boosting sales, having specific goals will shape your campaign strategy and guide your choices within the platform.

4. Enter Billing Information: Once you've signed in, provide your billing details. This ensures that you can easily manage your advertising expenses and unlock the full potential of Google Ads.

5. Set Up Your First Campaign: Now comes the exciting part – setting up your first campaign! Follow the guided steps within Google Ads to create your campaign. Choose the campaign type that aligns with your goals, such as Search, Display, Video, or Shopping campaigns.

6. Define Targeting and Budget: Tailor your audience targeting based on factors like demographics, location, interests, and keywords. Specify your daily or monthly budget to control your spending, ensuring you stay within your desired advertising limits.

7. Craft Engaging Ads: With your campaign structure in place, it's time to create compelling ads. Write captivating ad copy, select eye-catching visuals, and include relevant keywords that resonate with your audience.

8. Optimize Landing Pages: Ensure that your ads direct users to relevant and engaging landing pages on your website. A seamless user experience enhances the chances of conversions and boosts your campaign's success.

9. Monitor and Refine: After launching your campaign, closely monitor its performance. Analyze key metrics, such as click-through rates (CTR) and conversion rates, to identify areas for improvement. Make data-driven adjustments to optimize your ads and maximize results.

10. Continuous Learning and Iteration: Embrace the iterative nature of digital advertising. Stay informed about Google Ads updates, industry trends, and your target audience's preferences. Continuously test and experiment with different ad variations to discover what works best for your business.

As you progress on your Google Ads journey, remember that success often comes with patience and persistence. Stay committed to refining your strategies, learning from your experiences, and leveraging the platform's powerful tools to unlock the full potential of Google Ads for your business growth. Happy advertising!

* * *

CHAPTER 2: KEYWORD RESEARCH AND TARGETING

Conducting Keyword Research

Conducting keyword research on Google Ads is an essential step to ensure your ad campaigns reach the right audience and generate meaningful results. Here's an original guide to help you get started:

1. Define Your Focus: Begin by identifying the core themes or topics relevant to your business, products, or services. Think about what your potential customers might search for when looking for offerings similar to yours. This initial brainstorming will serve as the foundation for your keyword research.

2. Utilize Google's Keyword Planner: Access the powerful Google Ads Keyword Planner tool. Input your core themes or topics, and the tool will generate a comprehensive list of related keywords along with valuable insights, such as search volume and competition level.

3. Analyze Search Intent: Pay close attention to the search intent behind the keywords. Are users looking for information, products to purchase, or solutions to their problems? Understanding search intent will help you align your ads with users' specific needs and motivations.

4. Target Long-tail Keywords: Consider incorporating long-tail keywords into your research. These are longer, more specific keyword phrases that may have lower search volumes but often indicate higher intent and better

conversion potential. Long-tail keywords can help you reach a more qualified audience.

5. Competitor Research: Study your competitors' ads and websites to identify keywords they are targeting. Tools like SEMrush or SpyFu can provide valuable insights into their paid and organic search strategies, giving you a competitive edge.

6. Filter and Prioritize: Sort through the generated keyword list based on relevance, search volume, and competition. Focus on keywords that align closely with your business objectives and have the potential to drive meaningful traffic to your website.

7. Negative Keywords: Equally important is identifying negative keywords – terms that you don't want your ads to appear for. This helps avoid irrelevant clicks and optimizes your budget for the most relevant searches.

8. Group Keywords Strategically: Organize your keywords into thematic groups, also known as ad groups. This grouping allows you to create targeted ad copy and landing pages, ensuring a cohesive and relevant user experience.

9. Monitor and Refine: Keyword research is an ongoing process. Regularly analyze the performance of your selected keywords and make adjustments as needed. Add new keywords that emerge, and eliminate underperforming ones to continually optimize your campaigns.

10. Leverage Match Types: When setting up your keywords, make use of different match types (broad match, phrase match, exact match) to control the reach of your ads and increase their relevancy.

Remember, keyword research is not a one-time task; it's a dynamic and iterative process. Stay attuned to changing trends, user behavior, and industry dynamics to ensure your Google Ads campaigns remain effective and aligned with your business goals. Happy researching!

Choosing The Right Keywords For Your Campaigns

Selecting the right keywords for your Google Ads campaigns is crucial to reaching your target audience effectively and maximizing the return on your advertising investment. Here are some original tips to ensure you make informed decisions:

1. Understand Your Audience: Gain a deep understanding of your target audience - their preferences, pain points, and how they search for products or services like yours. This empathy-driven approach will guide you in selecting keywords that resonate with your potential customers.

2. Balance Relevance and Volume: Aim for keywords that strike the right balance between relevance to your offerings and an adequate search volume. Highly relevant keywords may have lower search volumes but are more likely to attract engaged and interested users.

3. Long-tail Keywords: Don't overlook the power of long-tail keywords. While they may have lower search volumes, they often indicate higher intent and can lead to more conversions. Embrace these specific phrases to capture the attention of a focused audience.

4. Use Keyword Planner and Tools: Leverage Google Ads' Keyword Planner and third-party tools to explore keyword ideas, search volumes, and competition levels. These resources provide valuable insights to inform your keyword choices.

5. Analyze Search Intent: Focus on understanding the search intent behind the keywords you consider. Are users looking for information, seeking to make a purchase, or comparing options? Align your ad copy and landing pages to cater to the specific intent of the search.

6. Negative Keywords: Don't forget to include negative keywords. These are terms that are irrelevant to your offerings, and you want to avoid showing your ads for them. Negative keywords help refine your targeting and prevent wasteful clicks.

7. Review Competitor Keywords: Investigate your competitors' keywords and ads to gain insights into their strategies. While not all competitor keywords will be relevant to your goals, it can spark ideas and reveal potential gaps in your approach.

8. Test and Refine: Embrace a testing mindset. Start with a set of keywords, monitor their performance, and be ready to adjust. Regularly review your campaigns, add new keywords, and remove underperforming ones to optimize your efforts continuously.

9. Keyword Match Types: Utilize different match types (broad match, phrase match, exact match) to control how closely your ads match search queries. This allows you to fine-tune your targeting and reach the right audience segments.

10. Budget Allocation: Allocate your budget wisely based on the importance and potential of various keywords. High-value keywords may require more investment, while less competitive ones can be cost-effective additions to your campaigns.

Remember, the process of selecting the right keywords is not static. Stay vigilant to market changes, industry trends, and shifts in user behavior. Continually refine your keyword strategy to stay relevant, competitive, and compelling in the dynamic world of Google Ads. With a thoughtful and data-driven approach, you can set the stage for a successful and impactful advertising journey.

Understanding Match Types And Their Significance

Understanding match types in Google Ads is pivotal to optimizing your targeting and controlling how closely your ads match users' search queries.

Here's an original guide to help you grasp match types and their significance:

1. Broad Match: Broad match is the most extensive match type, allowing your ads to appear for variations, synonyms, misspellings, and related searches. While it offers broad exposure, it may also lead to irrelevant clicks. Use broad match when you want to cast a wide net and discover new keyword opportunities.

2. Modified Broad Match: By adding a "+" symbol before essential keywords within a broad match, you create modified broad match keywords. This option offers a balance between broad reach and increased control. Your ads will only trigger for searches that include the specified keywords.

3. Phrase Match: Phrase match enables your ads to appear when a user's search query contains the exact phrase or close variations of it. The phrase is enclosed in quotation marks. It provides more control than broad match and ensures your ads align closely with user intent.

4. Exact Match: As the name suggests, exact match ensures your ads show only for the exact search query or close variants. Place the keyword in brackets [ ] to designate it as an exact match. This match type delivers high precision, targeting users with a specific intent, but it may limit reach.

5. Negative Match: Negative match allows you to exclude specific keywords from triggering your ads. Use this match type to prevent your ads from showing for irrelevant or unrelated searches, thus optimizing your budget and targeting.
Significance:

1. Relevance and Control: Each match type offers a varying degree of control over your ad's visibility. By selecting the right match types, you strike a balance between reaching a broader audience and targeting specific user queries.

2. Optimizing Budget: Match types help you allocate your budget more efficiently. For high-value keywords, you might prefer exact match to ensure precise targeting, while using broad match to explore additional keyword opportunities.

3. Understanding User Intent: Different match types reveal insights into users' search behaviors and intent. By analyzing performance data, you can uncover which match types resonate best with your target audience.

4. Negative Keywords: Negative match types are vital for eliminating irrelevant searches, minimizing wasted clicks, and refining your targeting strategy. They enhance the relevancy of your ads and improve the overall quality of your campaigns.

5. Testing and Iteration: Experimenting with various match types allows you to assess their impact on your campaign's performance. Regularly review and refine your match type choices to adapt to market dynamics and changing user behaviors.

In essence, understanding match types empowers you to fine-tune your Google Ads campaigns, reaching the most relevant audience and optimizing your budget. By embracing a thoughtful combination of match types, you can craft a powerful advertising strategy that aligns with your objectives and maximizes the effectiveness of your campaigns.

* * *

CHAPTER 3: CREATING COMPELLING AD COPY

Writing Persuasive Ad Headlines And Descriptions

Crafting persuasive ad headlines and descriptions for Google Ads is a true art, as it requires capturing attention, sparking curiosity, and compelling users to take action. Here's an original guide to help you create compelling ad copy that drives results:

1. Know Your Audience: Understand your target audience's pain points, desires, and motivations. Tailor your ad headlines and descriptions to resonate with their needs, ensuring a personal connection that draws them in.

2. Be Clear and Concise: Keep your headlines and descriptions concise and to the point. Communicate the value proposition clearly, highlighting the benefits users can expect from your product or service.

3. Include Relevant Keywords: Incorporate relevant keywords in your ad copy to enhance relevance and visibility. Aligning your copy with users' search queries increases the likelihood of your ads being shown.

4. Highlight Unique Selling Points: Differentiate your offering from competitors by emphasizing your unique selling points. Showcase what makes your product or service stand out to pique curiosity and entice clicks.

5. Create a Sense of Urgency: Urgency encourages action. Incorporate phrases like "limited time offer," "act now," or "last chance" to prompt users to take immediate action and avoid missing out on your offer.

6. Appeal to Emotions: Trigger emotional responses through your ad copy. Use powerful language to evoke excitement, joy, or a sense of relief that your product or service can provide.

7. Use Numbers and Statistics: Incorporate specific numbers and statistics to add credibility and authority to your claims. Quantifying the benefits of your offering can be more persuasive than vague statements.

8. Test Different Variations: A/B test multiple ad headlines and descriptions to identify the most effective combinations. Continuously experiment with different phrasing, messaging, and calls-to-action to refine your approach.

9. Match Landing Page Content: Ensure that your ad copy aligns seamlessly with the content on your landing page. Consistency in messaging reinforces your value proposition and creates a smooth user experience.

10. Call-to-Action (CTA): Include a clear and compelling call-to-action that encourages users to take the desired action, whether it's making a purchase, signing up, or requesting more information.

11. Localize if Applicable: If your business serves specific locations, consider including location-based language to appeal to local users and reinforce your relevance.

12. Think Mobile: With a significant portion of Google searches coming from mobile devices, ensure your ad copy is concise, visually engaging, and easy to read on smaller screens.

Remember, the best ad copy is a balance of art and data. Continuously monitor the performance of your ad campaigns and be prepared to iterate and optimize your headlines and descriptions based on insights and user behavior. By crafting persuasive ad copy that resonates with your audience and aligns with their needs, you can drive engagement, clicks, and conversions for your Google Ads campaigns.

Incorporating Keywords Into Your Ad Copy

Incorporating keywords into your ad copy in Google Ads requires finesse, ensuring that your ads remain relevant and compelling to both users and search engines. Here's an original guide to help you seamlessly integrate keywords into your ad copy:

1. Natural Language Integration: Craft your ad copy in a way that feels natural and conversational. Avoid forcing keywords into sentences, as it can compromise readability and user experience. Instead, focus on conveying your message effectively while strategically placing keywords where they naturally fit.

2. Headline Priority: Prioritize placing your most important keywords in the ad headline. This prominent position immediately captures users' attention and signals relevance to their search queries.

3. Customize for Each Ad Group: Tailor your ad copy for each ad group to align with the specific keywords in that group. This level of customization ensures that your ads directly address the intent behind users' searches, enhancing relevancy.

4. Highlight Benefits with Keywords: Incorporate keywords into the benefits and unique selling points of your product or service. This not only reinforces relevance but also emphasizes how your offering meets users' needs.

5. Utilize Ad Extensions: Leverage ad extensions, such as Sitelink Extensions and Callout Extensions, to feature additional keywords and expand the scope of your ad copy. Extensions provide more space to showcase different facets of your business.

6. Mirror User Queries: When appropriate, use the exact keywords from users' search queries in your ad copy. This technique reinforces relevancy and mirrors users' intent, increasing the chances of clicks and conversions.

7. Dynamic Keyword Insertion: Consider using dynamic keyword insertion (DKI) when applicable. DKI automatically inserts users' search terms into your ad copy, creating highly personalized ads that speak directly to individual users.

8. Test Keyword Variations: Experiment with different variations of your keywords within your ad copy. This allows you to identify which phrasings resonate best with your audience and drive optimal performance.

9. Quality Over Quantity: While keywords are essential, focus on providing valuable and compelling content. Strive to create ad copy that informs, entices, and convinces users, rather than simply stuffing keywords.

10. Review Ad Guidelines: Familiarize yourself with Google Ads' guidelines on keyword usage and character limits. Adhering to these rules ensures that your ads are approved and displayed correctly.

11. User Intent First: Always prioritize addressing user intent in your ad copy. While keywords are crucial for visibility, understanding and meeting users' needs will ultimately drive engagement and conversions.

By artfully incorporating keywords into your ad copy while keeping the user experience in mind, you can create persuasive, relevant, and high-performing Google Ads that captivate your audience and deliver meaningful results. Remember, the key is striking the right balance between optimization and delivering a compelling message that resonates with your potential customers.

Optimizing Your Ad Extensions

Optimizing ad extensions in Google Ads can greatly improve the performance and visibility of your ads. Ad extensions provide additional information to potential customers and encourage them to engage with your ads. Here are some steps to optimize your ad extensions:

Choose Relevant Extensions: Start by selecting ad extensions that are relevant to your business and campaign goals. Google Ads offers several types of extensions, including Sitelink, Callout, Structured Snippet, Call, Message, Location, and Price extensions. Choose the ones that make sense for your business.

Highlight Key Information: Use ad extensions to showcase important details about your products or services. For example, Sitelink extensions can direct users to specific pages on your website, Callout extensions can highlight unique selling points, and Structured Snippet extensions can provide additional categories or features.

Use Descriptive Text: Craft clear and compelling text for your ad extensions. Make sure the text is concise and informative, conveying the value proposition of your business.

Test Different Variations: Create multiple variations of ad extensions to see which ones perform best. Google Ads allows you to set up multiple extensions for each campaign or ad group. Monitor the performance metrics (click-through rate, conversion rate, etc.) to determine which extensions are most effective.

Utilize Call Extensions: If your goal is to drive phone calls, use call extensions to display your phone number directly in the ad. You can also track calls as conversions to measure the effectiveness of this extension.

Location Extensions: If you have a physical business location, enable location extensions to show your address, a map, and directions to potential customers.

Review Ad Preview: Use the Ad Preview and Diagnosis tool in Google Ads to see how your extensions appear in search results. This can help you identify any issues and ensure that your extensions are displayed correctly.

Schedule Extensions: Consider scheduling your extensions to appear during specific times when your target audience is most active. This can help you maximize the impact of your extensions.

Monitor Performance: Regularly analyze the performance of your ad extensions. Look for patterns and insights to refine your strategy over time. Adjust or pause underperforming extensions and focus on those that drive the best results.

Leverage Automated Extensions: Google Ads also offers automated extensions that are generated based on your website content. While these can be useful, make sure to review and customize them to ensure accuracy and relevance.

Align with Landing Pages: Ensure that the landing pages linked from your extensions are consistent with the information provided in the extensions. This creates a seamless user experience and helps improve your Quality Score.

Remember that ad extensions are an ongoing optimization process. Regularly review and refine your extensions based on performance data to continually enhance the effectiveness of your Google Ads campaigns.

* * *

CHAPTER 4: CAMPAIGN SETTINGS AND BUDGETING

Structuring Your Campaigns Effectively

Structuring your Google Ads campaigns effectively lays the foundation for a successful and organized advertising journey. Here's an original guide to help you create a well-structured campaign:

1. Clear Campaign Objectives: Start by defining clear and specific campaign objectives. Whether it's driving website traffic, increasing sales, or boosting brand awareness, a well-defined goal will guide your campaign structure and optimization efforts.

2. Segment by Theme or Product: Organize your campaigns based on themes, products, or services. Each campaign should focus on a specific category to ensure targeted messaging and easy performance tracking.

3. Ad Groups for Granularity: Within each campaign, create ad groups that further segment your keywords and ads. This granular approach allows you to tailor ad copy and landing pages more precisely to user intent.

4. Relevant Keywords: Assign highly relevant keywords to each ad group. This helps ensure that your ads show for the most appropriate searches, increasing their relevance and click-through rates (CTR).

5. Customized Ad Copy: Tailor your ad copy for each ad group, incorporating keywords and speaking directly to users' needs. A

personalized message resonates better with your audience and boosts the chance of conversions.

6. Landing Page Alignment: Ensure your landing pages align closely with the ad group's keywords and ad copy. A seamless user experience from ad click to landing page encourages users to take the desired action.

7. Ad Extensions for Extra Information: Utilize ad extensions to provide additional information and calls-to-action. Extensions enhance your ad's visibility and offer more opportunities to showcase different aspects of your business.

8. Budget Allocation: Allocate your budget strategically across campaigns based on their priorities and potential. High-value campaigns may warrant more significant investments to maximize returns.

9. Location and Device Targeting: Leverage location and device targeting to refine your audience reach. Tailoring campaigns based on geographic locations and device preferences ensures you connect with the right users at the right time.

10. Regular Review and Optimization: Monitor campaign performance regularly and make data-driven adjustments. Identify top-performing campaigns, ad groups, and keywords to optimize your budget and focus on what drives results.

11. Test and Experiment: Embrace a culture of testing and experimentation. Continuously test different ad variations, ad extensions, and landing pages to discover what resonates best with your audience.

12. Quality Score Awareness: Keep an eye on your Quality Scores. High-quality scores result from relevant keywords, ad copy, and landing pages, leading to improved ad rankings and lower costs.

By thoughtfully structuring your Google Ads campaigns, you create a cohesive and targeted approach that aligns with your objectives and audience needs. A well-organized campaign structure allows you to optimize effectively, allocate resources wisely, and achieve a higher level of performance and success in your advertising endeavors.

Setting Campaign Budgets And Bidding Strategies

Setting campaign budgets and bidding strategies in Google Ads is a delicate balance between achieving your advertising goals and maximizing your return on investment. Here's an original guide to help you make informed decisions:

1. Define Clear Objectives: Start by defining your campaign objectives and determining the value you assign to each conversion or action. Understand your target cost per acquisition (CPA) or return on ad spend (ROAS) to set the foundation for your budget and bidding strategy.

2. Consider Historical Data: Analyze historical campaign data to identify trends, peak periods, and successful bidding strategies. This information provides valuable insights to guide your current budget allocation and bidding decisions.

3. Budget Based on Goals: Allocate your budget based on the importance of each campaign and its objectives. High-priority campaigns may require more significant investments, while lower-priority ones can have more conservative budgets.

4. Start Conservatively: When launching a new campaign, start with a conservative budget and bidding strategy. Gather data on performance and adjust accordingly to optimize your spending over time.

5. Flexible Budgets: Embrace flexible budgets that allow you to adapt to market changes and campaign performance. Google Ads' daily budget option can automatically adjust spending to maximize exposure on high-performing days.

6. Automated Bidding Options: Consider using Google's automated bidding options, such as Target CPA or Target ROAS. These machine-learning algorithms optimize bids in real-time to achieve your desired conversion goals more efficiently.

7. Manual Bidding for Control: If you prefer more control, opt for manual bidding. Set bids at the keyword or ad group level, allowing you to fine-tune your strategy based on your analysis and expertise.

8. Bid Adjustments: Utilize bid adjustments for specific factors that impact your campaign's performance, such as device, location, or time of day. This allows you to optimize bids based on the value of each segment.

9. Monitor and Adjust: Continuously monitor campaign performance and adjust budgets and bidding strategies based on data-driven insights. Be prepared to reallocate budgets to top-performing campaigns and keywords.

10. Experiment and Test: Embrace a culture of experimentation. Test different bidding strategies, such as maximizing clicks or enhancing conversion value, to find the most effective approach for your unique goals.

11. Balance Competition and Costs: Consider your industry's competitiveness and average cost-per-click (CPC) when setting your bids. Strike a balance between bidding competitively to maintain visibility while avoiding excessive spending.

12. Focus on Quality Score: Improve your ad's Quality Score through relevant keywords, ad copy, and landing pages. A higher Quality Score can lead to lower CPCs and more favorable ad rankings.

Remember that campaign budgets and bidding strategies are not set in stone. Regularly assess your campaign's performance, adapt to changing market dynamics, and be open to refining your approach. With a strategic and data-driven approach, you can optimize your Google Ads campaigns for success and achieve your advertising objectives effectively.

Configuring Targeting Options For Better Reach

Configuring targeting options effectively in Google Ads is the key to expanding your reach and connecting with the right audience. Here's an original guide to help you optimize your targeting for better ad reach:

1. Understand Your Audience: Begin by understanding your target audience's demographics, interests, and behaviors. This insight allows you to align your targeting options with the preferences and characteristics of your potential customers.

2. Location Targeting: Leverage location targeting to reach users in specific geographic areas. Whether it's targeting a local audience or expanding to international markets, refining your location settings ensures your ads appear where they matter most.

3. Device Targeting: Tailor your campaigns to different devices such as mobile, desktop, and tablets. Device targeting enables you to optimize your ad experience for each platform and capitalize on user behaviors unique to each device.

4. Language Targeting: Choose the languages in which your ads will appear. Language targeting ensures that your message reaches users who understand and engage with your ad content.

5. Custom Intent and Affinity Audiences: Utilize custom intent and affinity audiences to reach users who have demonstrated specific interests or intents related to your offerings. This option expands your reach to users with relevant behaviors and online engagement.

6. Remarketing: Implement remarketing campaigns to re-engage users who have interacted with your website previously. Remarketing allows you to stay top-of-mind and bring back potential customers who have shown interest in your products or services.

7. Demographic Targeting: Refine your audience by demographic factors such as age, gender, and household income. Demographic targeting helps you reach users who align with your buyer personas, refining your ad reach to the most relevant audience.

8. Keyword Targeting: Use keyword targeting to show your ads when users search for specific terms or phrases. Strategic keyword selection ensures your ads appear in front of users actively seeking products or information related to your offerings.

9. Placement Targeting: Opt for placement targeting to display your ads on specific websites, YouTube channels, or mobile apps. This option allows you to reach users where they spend time online, ensuring your ads are contextually relevant.

10. Exclude Irrelevant Audiences: Implement negative targeting to exclude specific audiences or topics where your ads shouldn't appear. This helps prevent wasted ad spend on users unlikely to convert.

11. Experiment and Optimize: Continuously experiment with different targeting options to identify what resonates best with your audience. Monitor performance metrics and optimize your targeting settings based on data-driven insights.

12. Combine Targeting Options: Consider combining multiple targeting options for more refined reach. By layering location, interest, and keyword targeting, you can create a highly targeted and effective advertising approach.

By configuring your targeting options thoughtfully and strategically, you can extend the reach of your Google Ads campaigns to a relevant and engaged audience. Embrace a data-driven approach, regularly analyze performance metrics, and be willing to adapt your targeting strategies to achieve optimal results for your advertising endeavors.

* * *

CHAPTER 5: MONITORING AND OPTIMIZING CAMPAIGN PERFORMANCE

Understanding Key Performance Metrics

Understanding key performance metrics for Google Ads is essential for evaluating the effectiveness of your campaigns and making informed decisions to optimize your advertising efforts. Here's an original guide to help you grasp these metrics effectively:

1. Align Metrics with Objectives: Begin by aligning your key performance metrics with your campaign objectives. Define what success looks like for your business, whether it's driving conversions, increasing website traffic, or raising brand awareness.

2. Focus on Core Metrics: Pay attention to the core metrics that directly impact your goals. For conversions, track metrics like Conversion Rate, Cost per Conversion, and Conversion Value. For awareness, monitor metrics like Impressions, Click-Through Rate (CTR), and Reach.

3. Quality Score Matters: Keep an eye on Quality Score, as it affects your ad rankings and costs. A higher Quality Score can lead to lower Cost per Click (CPC) and improved ad positions, ultimately influencing your campaign's success.

4. Click-Through Rate (CTR): CTR indicates how often users click on your ads after seeing them. A high CTR suggests that your ads are relevant and engaging to your target audience.

5. Cost per Click (CPC): Understand your CPC to assess how much you pay for each click. Balancing CPC with the value of conversions ensures a cost-effective and efficient ad strategy.

6. Conversion Rate: Conversion Rate measures the percentage of clicks that result in a conversion. A higher conversion rate indicates a more effective ad and landing page experience.

7. Return on Investment (ROI): Calculate ROI to evaluate the profitability of your campaigns. Analyze the revenue generated against your advertising costs to determine the campaign's success.

8. Time Frame Matters: Consider the time frame when analyzing metrics. Assess short-term performance for quick adjustments, but also look at long-term trends to identify seasonality or changes in user behavior.

9. Segment Performance: Break down performance metrics by different segments, such as devices, locations, or ad groups. This analysis helps identify areas of strength and areas that need improvement.

10. Compare to Benchmarks: Compare your performance metrics to industry benchmarks or your past campaign results. This benchmarking provides valuable context and helps you set realistic goals for improvement.

11. A/B Testing: Conduct A/B tests to compare different ad variations and landing pages. This experimentation allows you to identify which elements drive better performance.

12. Continuously Optimize: Use performance metrics as a compass to guide your optimization efforts. Make data-driven adjustments to improve underperforming campaigns and capitalize on high-performing ones.

By mastering key performance metrics, you gain valuable insights into your Google Ads campaigns, allowing you to measure success, identify opportunities, and drive continual improvements. Adopt a holistic approach, regularly assess metrics, and be agile in adapting your strategies to achieve outstanding results in your advertising endeavors.

Analyzing Campaign Data And Making Data-Driven Decisions

Analyzing campaign data and making data-driven decisions for Google Ads is the compass that guides you toward advertising success. Here's an original guide to help you navigate this data-driven journey:

1. Establish Clear Objectives: Begin by defining clear campaign objectives and key performance indicators (KPIs). Align your data analysis with these goals to stay focused on what matters most for your business.

2. Data Collection and Organization: Ensure you have the right tracking mechanisms in place to collect accurate and comprehensive campaign data. Organize this data systematically, making it easily accessible for analysis.

3. Set a Baseline: Establish a baseline by analyzing historical performance data. This baseline provides a reference point for future comparisons and helps you identify trends and patterns.

4. Focus on Relevant Metrics: Concentrate on metrics directly tied to your campaign objectives. For instance, if your goal is conversions, closely monitor Conversion Rate, Cost per Conversion, and Conversion Value.

5. Segment and Compare: Segment your data to compare the performance of different campaigns, ad groups, or keywords. This segmentation allows you to identify top-performing segments and areas that need improvement.

6. A/B Testing for Insights: Conduct A/B tests with different ad variations, landing pages, or targeting options. Analyze the results to discover which

elements resonate best with your audience and drive higher engagement.

7. Benchmarking: Compare your campaign data to industry benchmarks or your previous performance to gain valuable context. Benchmarking highlights areas where you excel and areas that require attention.

8. Identify Trends and Patterns: Look for trends and patterns in your data over time. Seasonal trends or changes in user behavior can inform your campaign strategies and budget allocations.

9. Correlation vs. Causation: Distinguish between correlation and causation when analyzing data. Understand that two metrics may be related without one directly causing the other.

10. Data Visualization: Utilize data visualization tools to present complex data in a visually appealing and easy-to-understand manner. Visual representations help you spot trends and insights more efficiently.

11. Make Incremental Changes: Based on data analysis, make small and incremental changes to your campaigns. Measure the impact of these changes before making significant adjustments.

12. Embrace Agility: Be ready to adapt your strategies based on data-driven insights. Embrace an agile approach that allows you to respond to market dynamics and optimize your campaigns in real-time.

Data-driven decisions form the bedrock of successful Google Ads campaigns. Embrace a curious and analytical mindset, continuously monitor your data, and let it guide your optimization efforts. By combining creativity with evidence-based strategies, you can achieve remarkable results and unlock the full potential of Google Ads for your business growth.

Implementing Optimization Techniques To Improve Performance

Implementing optimization techniques is vital for improving performance on Google Ads and driving meaningful results for your advertising efforts. Here's an original guide to help you optimize your campaigns effectively:

1. Data-Driven Analysis: Base your optimization decisions on data analysis. Regularly review campaign metrics, identify patterns, and draw insights to understand what's working and what needs improvement.

2. Set Clear Goals: Define specific and measurable goals for your campaigns. Whether it's increasing conversions, improving click-through rates, or maximizing ROI, clear goals provide a roadmap for optimization efforts.

3. Focus on High-Performing Keywords: Identify top-performing keywords and allocate more budget and bidding efforts to maximize their impact. Conversely, pause or adjust bids for underperforming keywords.

4. Refine Ad Copy: Continuously test and refine ad copy to improve relevance and engagement. A/B test different variations to discover the most compelling messaging that resonates with your target audience.
5. Leverage Ad Extensions: Utilize ad extensions to enhance your ad's visibility and provide additional information to users. Extensions like Sitelinks, Callout Extensions, and Structured Snippets can boost click-through rates and conversions.

6. Optimize Landing Pages: Ensure that your landing pages align with your ad copy and provide a seamless user experience. Improve page load times, clarity of the call-to-action, and mobile responsiveness to increase conversion rates.

7. Geographic Targeting: Analyze location performance data and adjust bids based on the performance of different geographic areas. Tailor your targeting to focus on high-converting regions and adjust bids accordingly.

8. Device Optimization: Review performance data for different devices (mobile, desktop, tablet) and optimize bids based on their individual

conversion rates and value. Tailor your ads to provide an optimal experience on each device.

9. Ad Schedule Optimization: Analyze performance based on the time of day and day of the week. Adjust your ad schedule to maximize visibility during peak times when your target audience is most active.
10. Leverage Audience Insights: Utilize audience insights to understand the interests and behaviors of your website visitors. Implement remarketing and create custom audiences to re-engage and convert previous site visitors.

11. Bid Strategies: Explore automated bidding strategies, such as Target CPA or Target ROAS, to optimize bids based on your desired outcomes. These machine-learning algorithms adjust bids in real-time to meet your objectives efficiently.

12. Continuous Testing: Embrace a culture of continuous testing and experimentation. Test different ad elements, bidding strategies, and landing page variations to discover what drives the best results

.

Remember, optimization is an ongoing process. Regularly monitor your campaigns, stay informed about industry trends, and be prepared to adapt your strategies based on data insights. By combining creativity, data analysis, and strategic thinking, you can unlock the full potential of Google Ads and achieve outstanding performance for your advertising campaigns.

* * *

CHAPTER 6: AD FORMATS AND EXTENSIONS

Exploring Different Ad Formats (Text, Display, Video, Etc.)

Exploring different ad formats for Google Ads opens up a world of creative possibilities to effectively engage your audience. Here's an original guide to help you navigate and leverage various ad formats:

1. Research Google Ads Formats: Begin by familiarizing yourself with the diverse ad formats available on Google Ads. From Search Ads and Display Ads to Video Ads and Shopping Ads, each format offers unique strengths to suit different campaign goals.

2. Consider Your Campaign Objectives: Align ad formats with your specific campaign objectives. If you aim to boost brand awareness, Display Ads or Video Ads might be ideal. For driving conversions, consider Search Ads or Shopping Ads.

3. Experiment with Responsive Search Ads: Harness the power of Responsive Search Ads that adapt to users' search queries. Create multiple headlines and descriptions, and Google's algorithm dynamically combines them for the most relevant ad.

4. Engage with Display Ads: Utilize visually captivating Display Ads to showcase your brand across the Google Display Network. Incorporate

compelling images, enticing copy, and strong calls-to-action to attract users' attention.

5. Tell Your Story with Video Ads: Embrace Video Ads on platforms like YouTube to tell your brand's story or demonstrate products and services creatively. Keep videos concise, engaging, and aligned with your brand identity.

6. Showcase Products with Shopping Ads: Utilize Google Shopping Ads to display your products directly in search results. High-quality images and product details enhance the appeal and entice users to click.

7. Experiment with App Promotion Ads: If you have a mobile app, explore App Promotion Ads to drive app installs or encourage users to engage with your app's features.

8. Test Ad Extensions: Enhance your ad's visibility and engagement by using ad extensions such as Sitelinks, Callout Extensions, and Structured Snippets. These extensions provide additional information and calls-to-action.

9. Create Compelling Landing Pages: Regardless of the ad format, ensure your landing pages are relevant and compelling. Align them with your ad copy and offer a seamless user experience to boost conversions.

10. Optimize for Mobile: As mobile usage continues to rise, ensure your ad formats are optimized for mobile devices. Responsive design and mobile-friendly experiences are crucial for engaging mobile users effectively.

11. Use Dynamic Ads: Implement dynamic ad formats to show personalized content to users based on their previous interactions with your website. Dynamic ads enhance relevance and drive better engagement.

12. Monitor Performance and Iterate: Regularly analyze the performance of different ad formats. Identify top-performing formats and optimize underperforming ones. Continuously experiment and iterate based on data-driven insights.

Leveraging Ad Extensions To Enhance Your Ads

Leveraging ad extensions in your Google Ads allows you to make your ads more informative, engaging, and compelling to users, increasing their visibility and effectiveness. Here's an original guide to help you harness the power of ad extensions:

1. Enhance Relevance: Use ad extensions to provide additional context and relevance to your ads. Extensions, such as Sitelinks and Callout Extensions, enable you to showcase specific offerings, promotions, or key selling points directly in your ad.

2. Increase Click-Through Rates (CTR): Ad extensions can significantly boost CTR by expanding the real estate of your ad on the search results page. This increased visibility attracts more attention and entices users to click on your ad.

3. Showcase Products with Structured Snippets: Utilize Structured Snippets to highlight different product categories, services, or features. These snippets provide a quick overview, giving users a preview of what you offer before they click.

4. Location and Call Extensions: If you have a physical storefront, utilize Location Extensions to display your business address and help users find you easily. For mobile users, implement Call Extensions to encourage direct phone calls to your business.

5. Boost Mobile Performance: With mobile searches on the rise, extensions like Call Extensions and Message Extensions offer convenient ways for users to engage with your business directly from their mobile devices.

6. Dynamic Sitelinks: Employ Dynamic Sitelinks to automatically generate relevant and up-to-date links to various pages on your website. This ensures that users see the most relevant landing pages based on their search intent.

7. Social Proof with Review Extensions: Build trust and credibility by showcasing positive reviews and accolades with Review Extensions. Social proof can influence users' decisions and increase the likelihood of conversions.

8. App Promotion with App Extensions: If you have a mobile app, promote it with App Extensions to drive app installs and encourage users to interact with your app's features.

9. Use Callout Extensions for USPs: Highlight unique selling points (USPs) and key benefits of your products or services with Callout Extensions. This extra text space allows you to stand out from competitors and capture users' interest.

10. Regularly Update Extensions: Keep your extensions up-to-date, especially when running promotions or seasonal offers. Fresh and relevant extensions maintain the accuracy of your ad information.

11. A/B Test Extensions: Experiment with different combinations of ad extensions to identify which ones resonate best with your audience. A/B testing helps you determine the most effective extensions for your campaign goals.

12. Monitor Performance and Optimize: Continuously monitor the performance of your ad extensions. Focus on extensions that contribute positively to your campaign's goals and refine or pause those with lower impact.

By leveraging ad extensions strategically, you can create more engaging and informative Google Ads that capture users' attention, increase clicks, and drive better results for your advertising efforts. Each extension serves a unique purpose, and by understanding your audience and campaign goals, you can select the most relevant ones to elevate the effectiveness of your Google Ads.

Adapting Your Ad Formats For Different Devices

Adapting your ad formats for different devices is crucial for delivering a seamless and optimized user experience on Google Ads. Here's an original guide to help you tailor your ad formats effectively:

1. Responsive Design: Embrace responsive design principles to ensure that your ad formats automatically adjust to fit various screen sizes and resolutions. This approach delivers a consistent and user-friendly experience across all devices.

2. Mobile-First Mindset: Prioritize mobile users by creating ad formats with a mobile-first mindset. As mobile searches continue to rise, ensuring your ads are visually appealing and easy to interact with on mobile devices is paramount.

3. Short and Compelling Copy: Craft ad copy that is concise, yet compelling. Capture users' attention quickly, especially on mobile devices with limited screen space. Highlight the most essential information and calls-to-action upfront.

4. Visual Appeal: Use visually engaging images and graphics that resonate with your target audience. Ensure these visuals load quickly and maintain clarity on all devices, enhancing the overall impact of your ad formats.

5. Landing Page Optimization: Optimize your landing pages for mobile responsiveness and load times. Direct users to pages that are easy to navigate and interact with on mobile devices, creating a seamless transition from ad to landing page.

6. CTAs for Each Device: Tailor your calls-to-action (CTAs) based on the device. Consider using device-specific CTAs like "Call Now" for mobile users and "Learn More" for desktop users to maximize engagement.

7. Device-Specific Ad Extensions: Leverage device-specific ad extensions to provide relevant information and calls-to-action. For mobile users, use Call Extensions and Location Extensions to encourage direct calls and visits.

8. Test on Different Devices: Test your ad formats on various devices to ensure they render correctly and deliver an optimal user experience. This testing allows you to identify and address any issues or inconsistencies.

9. Performance Analysis: Analyze performance data for each device separately. Identify patterns and trends in user behavior, allowing you to make data-driven decisions for device-specific optimization.
10. Location Targeting: Utilize location targeting to tailor your ad formats for users in specific locations.
Customizing ads based on local preferences can enhance relevance and improve engagement.

11. Loading Speed: Optimize loading speed for all ad elements, such as images and landing pages. Fast-loading ads are crucial for retaining users' attention and preventing potential drop-offs.

12. Monitor and Iterate: Continuously monitor performance and adapt your ad formats based on user feedback and behavior. Be agile in making iterative improvements to deliver a seamless experience across all devices.

By adapting your ad formats for different devices, you create a cohesive and user-centric advertising approach. Prioritize mobile users, test your formats, and optimize based on performance insights to ensure your Google Ads effectively connect with your audience, regardless of the device they use.

* * *

CHAPTER 7: DISPLAY AND VIDEO ADVERTISING

Introduction To Display Advertising On The Google Display Network

Utilizing display advertising on the Google Display Network opens up vast opportunities to showcase your brand, products, and services to a diverse and engaged audience. Here's an original guide to help you leverage the power of display advertising effectively:

1. Define Your Target Audience: Start by clearly defining your target audience. Understand their demographics, interests, and behaviors to tailor your display ads for maximum relevance and impact.

2. Visual Appeal: Create visually captivating ads that grab users' attention. High-quality images, compelling graphics, and clear messaging can entice users to engage with your display ads.

3. Responsive Ad Design: Embrace responsive ad design to ensure your ads adapt seamlessly to different screen sizes and devices. This approach enables a consistent and user-friendly experience across the Display Network.

4. Leverage Remarketing: Utilize remarketing to reconnect with users who have previously visited your website. Remarketing ads can reinforce your

brand message and encourage users to revisit and convert.

5. Contextual Targeting: Use contextual targeting to display your ads on websites related to your products or services. This method ensures that your ads appear in contexts that align with users' interests.
6. Placement Targeting: Handpick specific websites, apps, or placements where you want your ads to appear. Placement targeting allows you to control the context and environment in which your ads are displayed.

7. Custom Affinity and Intent Audiences: Create custom affinity and intent audiences to reach users who have demonstrated specific interests or purchase intent related to your offerings. This targeting approach narrows your focus to highly relevant audiences.

8. Frequency Capping: Set frequency caps to control how often users see your ads. Avoid overwhelming your audience with excessive ad impressions, which could lead to ad fatigue.

9. Engaging Ad Formats: Experiment with engaging ad formats like interactive banners, video ads, and carousel ads to showcase your products or tell your brand story in a more dynamic and captivating way.

10. Optimize Landing Pages: Ensure that your landing pages align with the ad's messaging and offer a seamless transition from ad to website. An optimized landing page experience enhances the chances of conversions.

11. Test and Optimize: Continuously test different ad variations, targeting options, and creatives to identify what resonates best with your audience. Use performance data to optimize your campaigns for better results.

12. Monitor Performance Metrics: Regularly monitor key performance metrics such as click-through rates (CTR), conversion rates, and return on investment (ROI). These insights help you measure the success of your display advertising efforts.

By embracing the Google Display Network, you can amplify your brand's reach and engage with a diverse audience across websites, apps, and platforms. Customized targeting, visually appealing creatives, and strategic optimization will ensure your display ads capture users' attention and drive meaningful results for your advertising endeavors.

Creating Engaging Display And Video Ads

Creating engaging display and video ads in Google Ads requires a thoughtful approach that captivates your audience and drives action. Here's an original guide to help you craft compelling ads that leave a lasting impression:

1. Know Your Audience: Understand your target audience's preferences, interests, and pain points. Tailor your ad content to resonate with their needs, aspirations, and values.

2. Visual Storytelling: Use visuals to tell a compelling story. Whether through images or video, convey your brand's narrative in a way that evokes emotions and connects with viewers on a deeper level.

3. Keep it Concise: Deliver your message concisely and effectively. Capture attention early on, as users have limited time and patience online. Make every second count.

4. Highlight Benefits: Focus on the benefits of your products or services. Clearly communicate how they solve problems or enhance the lives of your customers.

5. Clear Call-to-Action (CTA): Include a strong and clear CTA that guides viewers on what action to take next. Use action-oriented language to encourage engagement.

6. Optimize for Mobile: Ensure your ads are optimized for mobile devices, considering the rising mobile usage. Keep text readable and visuals clear on smaller screens.

7. Experiment with Ad Formats: Test different ad formats such as interactive banners, carousel ads, and video ads. Variety keeps your ads fresh and captures attention in unique ways.

8. Personalization: Incorporate personalized elements in your ads, such as using the viewer's name or location. Personalization enhances relevance and engagement.

9. Showcase USPs: Highlight your Unique Selling Propositions (USPs) prominently. Differentiate your brand from competitors and communicate what sets you apart.

10. Embrace Creativity: Don't be afraid to think outside the box. Unconventional and creative ideas can make your ads stand out and be memorable.

11. A/B Test Continuously: Run A/B tests with different ad variations to identify what performs best. Test visuals, headlines, CTAs, and even different story angles to optimize your ads' effectiveness.

12. Optimize Landing Pages: Ensure your landing pages align with the ad's message and design. A seamless user experience from ad click to landing page enhances conversions.

By employing these strategies, you can create engaging display and video ads that resonate with your audience, effectively convey your brand's value, and drive meaningful interactions. Embrace creativity, continuously optimize based on data-driven insights, and never stop exploring new ways to connect with your target audience through Google Ads.

Targeting And Optimizing Display And Video Campaigns

Targeting and optimizing display and video campaigns in Google Ads require a strategic and data-driven approach to maximize their impact and reach. Here's an original guide to help you achieve exceptional results:

1. Audience Segmentation: Segment your target audience based on demographics, interests, behaviors, and past interactions. Leverage custom affinity and intent audiences to focus on users with specific affinities and purchase intent relevant to your offerings.

2. Contextual Relevance: Use contextual targeting to display your ads on websites and placements related to your products or services. Aligning your ads with relevant content enhances engagement and resonates with users' interests.

3. Remarketing and Exclusions: Implement remarketing campaigns to re-engage users who have interacted with your brand previously. Also, exclude audiences who have already converted to optimize your ad spend.

4. Frequency Capping: Set frequency caps to control how often users see your ads. Avoid overwhelming your audience with excessive ad impressions, which could lead to ad fatigue.

5. Location Targeting: Optimize your campaigns with location targeting. Tailor your ads for different geographic regions to address local preferences and boost relevance.

6. Ad Scheduling: Analyze performance data to determine peak times for engagement. Schedule your ads strategically to maximize visibility during high-converting hours.

7. Creative Optimization: A/B test different ad creatives, headlines, and calls-to-action to discover what resonates best with your audience. Optimize your visuals and messaging based on performance insights.

8. Leverage Responsive Ads: Use responsive ad formats that automatically adjust to fit various screen sizes and devices. Responsive ads ensure a seamless user experience across different platforms.

9. Monitor Video Ad Metrics: Track video ad metrics such as view-through rate, play rate, and engagement rate to assess video performance. Optimize

videos based on audience retention and engagement data.

10. Optimize Landing Pages: Ensure that your landing pages align with the ad's message and design. A cohesive experience from ad click to landing page improves user satisfaction and conversions.
11. Test Different Bidding Strategies: Experiment with different bidding strategies, such as target CPA or target ROAS, to optimize for your campaign goals. Choose the bidding strategy that aligns with your objectives.

12. Analyze Performance Data: Continuously analyze performance data to identify strengths and areas for improvement. Use data-driven insights to make informed decisions and fine-tune your targeting and optimization efforts.

By combining precise targeting, creative optimization, and continuous analysis, you can elevate the effectiveness of your display and video campaigns in Google Ads. Stay agile, embrace experimentation, and adapt your strategies based on performance data to achieve remarkable results and reach your advertising goals.

* * *

CHAPTER 8: REMARKETING AND CONVERSION TRACKING

Implementing Remarketing Campaigns To Reach Previous Visitors

Implementing remarketing campaigns in Google Ads allows you to reconnect with previous website visitors and keep your brand top-of-mind. Here's an original guide to help you effectively set up remarketing campaigns:

1. Install Remarketing Tags: Begin by adding Google's remarketing tag to your website. This tag helps track visitors and creates custom audience lists for your remarketing campaigns.

2. Segment Your Audiences: Segment your remarketing audiences based on specific interactions or behaviors on your website. Create lists for different pages visited, actions taken, or products viewed to tailor your ads accordingly.

3. Create Engaging Ads: Craft compelling ad creatives that resonate with each audience segment. Personalize your ads based on users' previous interactions, showcasing relevant products or personalized messages.

4. Avoid Overwhelm: Set frequency caps to control how often users see your remarketing ads. Avoid overwhelming them with too many impressions, ensuring a positive user experience.

5. Cross-Sell and Upsell: Use remarketing to cross-sell or upsell to existing customers. Showcase complementary products or exclusive offers to entice them back to your website.

6. Abandoned Cart Recovery: Target users who abandoned their carts with remarketing ads. Remind them of the items left behind and incentivize them to complete their purchase.

7. Dynamic Remarketing: Implement dynamic remarketing to show personalized ads featuring products users previously viewed on your website. Dynamic ads enhance relevance and boost engagement.

8. Exclude Converted Users: Exclude users who have already completed a desired action, such as making a purchase or filling out a contact form. This prevents wasting ad spend on users who have already converted.

9. Create Time-Based Segments: Consider creating audience segments based on different time frames of website visits. Tailor your ads based on recency of interactions to capitalize on user interest.

10. Leverage Cross-Device Remarketing: Utilize cross-device remarketing to reach users across multiple devices. This ensures consistent messaging and maximizes touchpoints with your audience.

11. Test Different Ad Formats: Experiment with various ad formats, such as static images, animated banners, or video ads, to see which resonates best with your remarketing audiences.

12. Analyze and Optimize: Regularly analyze the performance of your remarketing campaigns. Measure engagement, conversions, and return on investment (ROI) to optimize bidding and ad creative.

By implementing remarketing campaigns thoughtfully, you can re-engage previous website visitors, nurture them through the customer journey, and drive valuable actions. Tailor your ads to suit specific audience segments, leverage dynamic remarketing, and continuously optimize based on performance insights to make the most of your remarketing efforts in Google Ads.

Tracking Conversions And Measuring Campaign Success

Tracking conversions and measuring campaign success in Google Ads is crucial for evaluating the effectiveness of your advertising efforts. Here's an original guide to help you best track conversions and measure success:

1. Set Clear Conversion Goals: Define clear and specific conversion goals for your campaigns. Whether it's purchases, sign-ups, form submissions, or other valuable actions, clarity in objectives helps focus your measurement efforts.

2. Implement Conversion Tracking: Install Google's conversion tracking code on your website to monitor user actions accurately. This code tracks when a user completes a conversion goal, attributing it back to the specific ad click.

3. Assign Values to Conversions: Assign values to different conversion actions based on their importance to your business. This allows you to measure the impact of your campaigns in terms of revenue or other key performance indicators (KPIs).

4. Track Multiple Conversion Types: Use Google Ads to track multiple conversion types, such as purchases and lead form submissions. Tracking multiple conversions provides a comprehensive view of campaign performance.

5. Attribution Models: Choose an attribution model that aligns with your business objectives. Attribution models determine how credit for conversions is assigned to different touchpoints in the user journey.

6. Analyze Conversion Data: Regularly analyze conversion data to assess campaign performance. Measure conversion rates, cost per conversion, and conversion value to gauge the efficiency of your campaigns.

7. Customize Conversion Windows: Customize the conversion window to match your business cycle. Some conversions may occur days or weeks after the initial ad interaction, and adjusting the window ensures accurate measurement.

8. Monitor Assisted Conversions: Assess the impact of your ads on the entire conversion funnel. Analyze assisted conversions to understand how your ads influence user decisions throughout their journey.

9. Integration with Analytics: Integrate Google Ads with Google Analytics to gain deeper insights into user behavior. This integration provides a holistic view of campaign performance and user interactions.

10. Set Up E-commerce Tracking: If you have an e-commerce website, enable e-commerce tracking to monitor specific transactions, revenue, and product performance directly within Google Ads.

11. Analyze Search Terms and Keywords: Analyze search terms and keyword data to understand which queries drive conversions. Optimize your campaigns based on this insight to increase conversions.

12. Continuous Optimization: Use conversion data to make data-driven decisions for campaign optimization. Regularly adjust bids, ad copy, and targeting to improve campaign performance over time.

By tracking conversions and measuring campaign success effectively, you gain valuable insights into your advertising performance. Understanding how your ads drive valuable actions enables you to make informed decisions, allocate budgets wisely, and optimize your Google Ads campaigns for exceptional results and business growth.

Setting Up Conversion Tracking For Various Goals

Setting up conversion tracking for various goals in Google Ads is essential for measuring the success of your advertising efforts. Here's an original step-by-step guide to help you get started:

1. Define Conversion Goals: Begin by defining specific conversion goals for your campaigns. Identify the key actions you want users to take on your website, such as purchases, sign-ups, form submissions, or downloads.

2. Create Conversion Actions: In your Google Ads account, navigate to "Tools & Settings" and select "Conversions." Click on the "+" button to create a new conversion action.

3. Select Conversion Type: Choose the appropriate conversion type based on your goal. Options include website, app, and phone call conversions. For website conversions, select "Website" and click "Continue."

4. Choose Conversion Category: Choose the appropriate conversion category that aligns with your goal. Categories include purchase/sale, sign-up, lead, or view of a key page. Select the relevant category and click "Continue."

5. Name and Value: Give your conversion action a descriptive name that reflects the specific action users take. Set a value for your conversion if applicable, such as a monetary amount for purchases. This helps measure the revenue generated by your campaigns.

6. Conversion Counting: Choose how you want conversions to be counted. Select "Every" if users can complete the conversion multiple times. Choose "One" if you want to count unique conversions per user.

7. Conversion Window: Set the conversion window to match your business cycle. The default is 30 days, but you can adjust it based on your specific

needs.

8. Include in "Conversions": Choose whether to include the conversion in "Conversions" reporting. This option allows you to include or exclude this conversion action from your primary conversion metrics.

9. Attribution Model: Select an attribution model that determines how credit for the conversion is assigned to different ad interactions. You can choose from various models, such as last click, first click, or data-driven attribution.

10. Install the Tracking Code: After customizing your settings, click "Create and Continue." You'll receive a tracking code that needs to be placed on the relevant pages of your website. Follow the provided instructions to install the code correctly.

11. Test Conversion Tracking: After installing the tracking code, conduct test conversions to ensure that the tracking is working correctly. Check the "Conversions" section in your Google Ads account to verify that the conversions are being recorded accurately.

12. Monitor and Optimize: Regularly monitor your conversion data in Google Ads to evaluate campaign performance. Use this data to optimize your bidding, targeting, and ad creatives for better results.

By following these steps, you can set up conversion tracking for various goals in Google Ads. Accurate conversion tracking enables you to measure the effectiveness of your campaigns, make data-driven decisions, and maximize the return on your advertising investment.

* * *

CHAPTER 9: ADVANCED STRATEGIES AND FEATURES

Exploring Advanced Campaign Settings And Features

Exploring advanced campaign settings and features in Google Ads empowers you to unlock new opportunities and optimize your advertising efforts. Here's an original guide to help you delve into these advanced options:

1. Ad Schedule Customization: Customize ad scheduling to target specific days and times when your audience is most active. This feature ensures your ads appear when they are most likely to drive conversions.

2. Device Bid Adjustments: Fine-tune your bids based on device performance. Adjust bids for mobile, desktop, and tablet devices to optimize for higher-converting platforms.

3. Location Targeting Options: Go beyond basic location targeting. Explore advanced location settings, such as radius targeting, location exclusions, or targeting specific locations with high potential.

4. Ad Rotation Settings: Choose from different ad rotation options, such as "Optimize" or "Rotate Indefinitely." Tailor your ad rotation settings to test different ad variations and find the most effective ones.

5. Audience Expansion: Utilize audience expansion to reach users with similar interests and behavior patterns as your existing remarketing or customer lists. This feature can widen your audience reach while maintaining relevance.

6. Campaign URL Options: Use campaign URL options to track specific parameters or attributes for your ads. These options enable better tracking and measurement of campaign performance.

7. IP Exclusions: Exclude specific IP addresses or IP ranges to prevent your ads from appearing to specific audiences or competitors in particular locations.

8. Custom Ad Scheduling: Implement custom ad scheduling to adjust bids during specific time frames, such as promotional periods or peak business hours.

9. Demographic Targeting: Explore demographic targeting options to narrow down your audience based on age, gender, or household income. This feature allows you to refine your targeting for better relevance.

10. Dynamic Search Ads: Embrace dynamic search ads to automatically generate ad headlines and landing pages based on your website content. This option simplifies ad creation and targets relevant keywords automatically.

11. Smart Bidding Strategies: Harness smart bidding strategies, such as Target CPA or Target ROAS, which utilize machine learning to optimize bids based on your desired outcomes.

12. Automated Extensions: Enable automated extensions to display additional relevant information with your ads automatically. These extensions, such as seller ratings or dynamic site links, enhance your ad's visibility and relevance.

By exploring these advanced campaign settings and features, you can tailor your Google Ads to your specific business objectives and gain a competitive edge. Continuously experiment, analyze performance, and optimize based on data-driven insights to achieve exceptional results and drive meaningful outcomes for your advertising efforts.

Implementing Advanced Bidding Strategies

Implementing advanced bidding strategies in Google Ads enables you to optimize your campaign performance and achieve your desired advertising goals more effectively. Here's an original guide to help you implement these strategies:

1. Understand Your Goals: Clearly define your campaign objectives and key performance indicators (KPIs). Whether it's maximizing conversions, increasing revenue, or achieving a specific target return on ad spend (ROAS), knowing your goals is crucial for choosing the right bidding strategy.

2. Smart Bidding Options: Explore Google's smart bidding options, such as Target CPA (Cost-Per-Acquisition), Target ROAS (Return on Ad Spend), or Enhanced CPC (Cost-Per-Click). These strategies leverage machine learning to optimize bids based on historical performance and user behavior.

3. Data-Driven Insights: Ensure your campaign has sufficient conversion data to leverage smart bidding effectively. The more data Google's algorithms have, the better they can optimize bids for your desired outcomes.

4. Test and Monitor: Start with conservative bids and gradually increase or decrease them based on performance. Continuously monitor the results and make adjustments to refine your bidding strategy.

5. Seasonal Adjustments: Consider making seasonal bid adjustments to accommodate fluctuations in user behavior and demand during peak periods or special occasions.

6. Customize Bid Strategies: Tailor your bidding strategies for different campaign goals or product categories. Utilize bid adjustments, such as device bid adjustments or location bid adjustments, to optimize bids based on specific factors.

7. Maximize Conversions: If your goal is to maximize conversions within a set budget, use the "Maximize Conversions" bidding strategy. This option automatically adjusts bids to get the most conversions possible.

8. Target Impression Share: Opt for the "Target Impression Share" strategy to increase your ad visibility. This bidding option aims to place your ads at the top of the search results page or to show them more often.

9. Manual CPC Bidding: For greater control over individual keyword bids, consider using manual CPC bidding. This strategy allows you to set bids manually for each keyword based on your desired performance.

10. Combine Strategies: Experiment with combining different bidding strategies within the same campaign or ad group. This hybrid approach can be effective for achieving diverse objectives simultaneously.

11. Adapt and Optimize: As your campaign progresses, analyze the performance data regularly. Adjust your bidding strategies based on data-driven insights to improve campaign efficiency and drive better results.

12. Budget Considerations: Be mindful of your budget constraints when implementing advanced bidding strategies. Ensure that your bids align with your budget and that you're maximizing the value of your ad spend.

By implementing advanced bidding strategies thoughtfully, you can enhance the effectiveness of your Google Ads campaigns. Whether it's optimizing for conversions, ROAS, or ad visibility, these strategies leverage automation and machine learning to drive meaningful outcomes for your advertising efforts. Stay proactive, experiment, and fine-tune your bidding approach to achieve exceptional results.

Leveraging Audience Targeting And Segmentation

Leveraging audience targeting and segmentation in Google Ads allows you to reach the right people with the right message, maximizing the impact of your advertising campaigns. Here's an original guide to help you harness the power of audience targeting:

1. Understand Your Audience: Start by understanding your target audience's demographics, interests, behaviors, and preferences. This knowledge forms the foundation for effective audience targeting.

2. Audience Insights: Utilize Google Analytics and other data sources to gain audience insights. Analyze user behavior on your website to identify high-performing segments and their characteristics.

3. Create Custom Audiences: Build custom audiences based on specific criteria. Use remarketing lists, customer lists, and website visitor data to create tailored audiences for your campaigns.

4. Segmentation Strategies: Segment your audience based on factors like purchase history, engagement level, or specific actions taken. Segmentation allows you to deliver personalized messages that resonate with each group.

5. In-Market Audiences: Target users who are actively researching products or services similar to yours with in-market audiences. This targeting option can increase the likelihood of conversions.

6. Affinity Audiences: Reach users with specific interests or passions relevant to your offerings using affinity audiences. These audiences are

interested in topics related to your products, making them more likely to engage.

7. Custom Intent Audiences: Leverage custom intent audiences to target users based on their recent search behavior. This targeting option allows you to reach users actively searching for products or services like yours.

8. Similar Audiences: Expand your reach by targeting similar audiences to your existing customer base. Google's algorithms identify users with similar characteristics to those on your customer lists.

9. Layered Targeting: Combine different audience targeting options with other targeting methods, such as keywords or demographics, to fine-tune your reach and relevance.

10. Exclude Audiences: Use negative audience targeting to exclude specific segments from seeing your ads. This ensures that your ads are shown to the most relevant audience, increasing ad efficiency.

11. A/B Testing: Conduct A/B testing to compare the performance of different audience segments. Analyze results to identify high-converting audiences and optimize your targeting accordingly.

12. Dynamic Ad Customization: Create dynamic ad content that adapts to different audience segments. Tailor your ad messaging to address the specific needs and preferences of each audience group.

By leveraging audience targeting and segmentation, you can deliver more personalized and relevant ads to your audience, increasing engagement and conversion rates. Understand your audience, create custom segments, and continuously analyze performance data to optimize your targeting strategies and achieve remarkable results with your Google Ads campaigns.

CHAPTER 10: A/B TESTING AND CONTINUOUS IMPROVEMENT

Understanding The Importance Of A/B Testing

Understanding the importance of A/B testing for Google Ads is pivotal to unlock the full potential of your advertising efforts. Here's an original guide to help you grasp the significance of A/B testing:

1. Data-Driven Decisions: A/B testing empowers you to make data-driven decisions rather than relying on assumptions. By testing different ad elements, you gain valuable insights into what resonates best with your audience.

2. Optimize Ad Performance: A/B testing allows you to optimize ad performance continuously. By comparing different variations, you can identify high-converting elements and refine your ads accordingly.

3. Maximize Return on Investment (ROI): A/B testing enables you to allocate your budget more effectively. By investing in ads with proven success, you maximize your ROI and achieve better results.

4. Iterative Improvement: Embrace A/B testing as an iterative process. Continuously refine your ads based on test results, leading to gradual improvements that result in higher performance over time.

5. Tailored Messaging: A/B testing lets you customize ad messaging to different audience segments. By understanding what appeals most to specific groups, you can deliver more relevant and persuasive messages.

6. Uncover Audience Preferences: Discover what your audience prefers through A/B testing. Whether it's different visuals, headlines, or calls-to-action, understanding these preferences helps you tailor future campaigns.

7. Stay Competitive: In the dynamic landscape of online advertising, A/B testing keeps you competitive. Constantly improving your ads ensures you stay relevant and engaging to your audience.

8. Adapt to Changing Trends: Consumer behavior and preferences evolve over time. A/B testing helps you adapt to changing trends, ensuring your ads remain effective and resonate with your audience.

9. Discover Unexpected Insights: Sometimes A/B testing uncovers unexpected insights that you may not have considered initially. These insights can lead to creative innovations that set your ads apart from the competition.

10. Optimize for Different Goals: A/B testing allows you to optimize ads for different campaign objectives, whether it's click-through rates, conversions, or engagement metrics.

11. Cost-Effective Testing: A/B testing is a cost-effective way to experiment with ad variations. Rather than rolling out major changes without validation, you can test small tweaks and measure their impact.

12. Continuous Growth: Embracing A/B testing as part of your advertising strategy fosters a culture of continuous growth and improvement. It encourages innovation and creativity while maintaining a focus on measurable results.

In summary, A/B testing is not just an option; it is a crucial practice for successful Google Ads campaigns. It empowers you to make informed decisions, optimize ad performance, and create tailored messages that resonate with your audience. By embracing A/B testing, you ensure your advertising efforts stay relevant, efficient, and geared towards achieving your goals.

Conducting Split Tests To Optimize Campaigns

Conducting split tests, also known as A/B tests, is a powerful way to optimize your campaigns on Google Ads. Here's an original step-by-step guide to help you effectively conduct split tests:

1. Identify Testing Objectives: Begin by defining clear testing objectives. Determine what specific elements you want to test, such as ad headlines, visuals, calls-to-action, or landing pages.

2. Create Test Variations: Develop different variations for the elements you want to test. For example, create multiple ad headlines or different visuals to compare performance.

3. Segment Your Audience: Segment your audience into groups, and randomly assign each group to a different test variation. Ensure the groups are of sufficient size to produce statistically significant results.

4. Run Simultaneous Tests: Run the split tests simultaneously to minimize external factors that could skew results. This ensures that the performance differences are attributed solely to the test variations.

5. Monitor and Measure: Monitor the performance of each test variation using Google Ads' reporting and analytics. Measure relevant metrics, such as click-through rates (CTR), conversion rates, and return on ad spend (ROAS).

6. Test Duration: Allow your split test to run for a sufficient duration to gather enough data. The duration may vary depending on your campaign's traffic volume, but aim for a timeframe that ensures statistical significance.

7. Statistical Significance: Ensure that the test results are statistically significant before drawing conclusions. You can use online statistical significance calculators to verify the significance of your results.

8. Choose the Winner: Based on the test results, identify the variation that performed better and achieved your testing objectives. This variation becomes the winner and should be implemented in your campaign.

9. Implement and Optimize: Implement the winning variation in your campaign, and continuously optimize based on the insights gained from the split test.

10. Iterative Testing: Embrace iterative testing to continually refine your campaign elements. Repeat the process by testing new variations to drive further improvements.

11. Single Variable Testing: Focus on testing one variable at a time to isolate its impact on performance. Testing multiple variables simultaneously can make it challenging to attribute changes to specific elements.

12. Keep Testing Regularly: Make split testing a regular part of your campaign optimization strategy. As your audience and market evolve, ongoing testing ensures your ads remain relevant and effective.

By conducting split tests methodically, you can fine-tune your Google Ads campaigns, optimize for better performance, and achieve your advertising objectives. Stay focused on clear testing goals, measure results accurately, and implement winning variations to drive continuous improvement in your campaigns.

Developing A Continuous Improvement Plan For Long-Term Success

Developing a continuous improvement plan is essential for achieving long-term success with your Google Ads campaigns. Here's an original guide to help you create a sustainable plan:

1. Set Clear Objectives: Define specific and measurable campaign objectives aligned with your overall business goals. Clearly outline what you want to achieve through your Google Ads efforts.

2. Analyze Performance Regularly: Regularly review campaign performance data to identify strengths, weaknesses, and areas for improvement. Use Google Ads reports and analytics to gain valuable insights.

3. Identify Key Metrics: Focus on key performance metrics that align with your objectives. Whether it's click-through rates (CTR), conversion rates, or return on ad spend (ROAS), understanding these metrics is crucial for tracking success.

4. Data-Driven Decision Making: Base your decisions on data rather than assumptions. Utilize A/B testing, performance data, and audience insights to inform your optimization strategies.

5. Optimize Ad Creatives: Continuously refine your ad creatives based on performance data. Test different headlines, visuals, and calls-to-action to uncover what resonates best with your audience.

6. Landing Page Optimization: Ensure your landing pages align with your ad messaging and offer a seamless user experience. Optimize landing pages to encourage conversions and enhance user satisfaction.
7. Budget Allocation: Regularly assess the performance of your budget allocation across campaigns. Shift budget to high-performing campaigns or ad groups to maximize return on investment.

8. Monitor Keyword Performance: Keep a close eye on keyword performance to identify which keywords are driving the most valuable traffic. Optimize bids and adjust keyword targeting accordingly.

9. Explore New Opportunities: Stay proactive in exploring new opportunities within Google Ads. Embrace different ad formats, audience targeting options, or emerging trends to expand your reach.

10. Competitor Analysis: Monitor your competitors' activities and strategies. Analyze their ad copy, keywords, and positioning to find areas where you can differentiate and improve.

11. Stay Updated with Google Ads Features: Keep yourself informed about the latest features and updates in Google Ads. Embracing new tools and functionalities can give you a competitive advantage.

12. Regular Reviews and Reporting: Schedule regular reviews of your continuous improvement plan's progress. Use the insights gained to adjust your strategies and refine your long-term approach.

Remember, continuous improvement is an ongoing process. Stay committed to refining your Google Ads campaigns, staying informed about industry trends, and implementing data-driven strategies. By fostering a culture of continuous learning and adaptation, you can achieve long-term success, drive sustainable growth, and stay ahead of the

competition in the dynamic world of online advertising.

CONCLUSION

Congratulations on completing "Fuel The Growth Of Your Brand: Your Guide To Mastering Google Ads." By now, you should have a solid understanding of how Google Ads works and how to create effective campaigns. Remember, digital advertising is an ever-evolving field, so stay curious, keep learning, and adapt your strategies to stay ahead. Good luck with your future Google Ads endeavors

And as an added bonus, scan the QR code below and get 10% off any t-shirt purchase. Simply apply the code BOOK at checkout.